GW00728895

F*^

UP

THIS

BOOK

(...not your life)

About the Author

Fred Calhoun is a novelist, footballer and adventurer. His list of successful ventures and achievements is too extensive to list here. No, hang on, these are his fantasy answers from p27.

In reality, the author earns a crust working in publishing and has a lovely family and two dogs, both of whom seem to like him more than most people do.

He admits he could probably use some therapy but is too tight to pay for it. So he decided to write this book for anyone who feels the same way but needs to let off a little steam from time to time.

F**K UP THIS BOOK

THIS BOOK

(...not your life)*

A SURPRISINGLY POINTLESS BOOK
FOR GROWN-UPS

FRED CALHOUN

* RECOMMENDED FOR GROWN-UPS WITH
MILD TO MODERATE EXISTENTIAL ANGST

BLACK & WHITE PUBLISHING

First published 2015
by Black & White Publishing Ltd
29 Ocean Drive, Edinburgh EH6 6JL

1 3 5 7 9 10 8 6 4 2   15 16 17 18

ISBN: 978 1 78530 002 8

Copyright © Fred Calhoun 2015

The right of Fred Calhoun to be identified as the author of this
work has been asserted by him in accordance with the Copyright,
Designs and Patents Act 1988.

All rights reserved. No part of this publication may be reproduced,
stored in a retrieval system, or transmitted in any form, or by
any means, electronic, mechanical, photocopying, recording or
otherwise, without permission in writing from the publisher.

The publisher has made every reasonable effort to contact
copyright holders of images in this book. Any errors are
inadvertent and anyone who for any reason has not been
contacted is invited to write to the publisher so that a full
acknowledgment can be made in subsequent editions of this work.

A CIP catalogue record for this book is available
from the British Library.

Typeset by www.RichardBuddDesign.co.uk
Printed and bound by Nørhaven, Denmark

CONTENTS

Dedication

To Philip 'they fuck you up, your mum and dad' Larkin, who opened many eyes to the dark forces at work in life.

FC

INTRODUCTION

F**K UP THIS BOOK (...NOT YOUR LIFE) IS THE ULTIMATE
ACTIVITY BOOK FOR GROWN-UPS OF ALL AGES, AND IS IDEAL
FOR ANYONE WITH MILD TO MODERATE EXISTENTIAL ANGST.

WE ALL HAVE THOSE DAYS, DON'T WE? WHEN THE TRAFFIC
LIGHTS TURN RED JUST BEFORE WE GET THERE AND JUST
TOO LATE TO STEP ON THE GAS AND SNEAK THROUGH ON
ORANGE. AND IT'S ALWAYS THE LONGEST LIGHT IN THE
WORLD. OR WHEN THE TRAIN STOPS IN THE MIDDLE OF
NOWHERE FOR AN AGE AND FOR NO OBVIOUS REASON WHEN
WE'RE ALREADY LATE FOR A MEETING. OR WHEN EVERYONE
YOU MEET OR TALK TO ON A GIVEN DAY PISSES YOU OFF.
THEN YOU GET HOME AND YOUR PARTNER SEEMS INTENT
ON WINDING YOU UP, OR THE KIDS WANT MORE STUFF, MORE
FOOD, MORE THINGS DONE. ALWAYS MORE. NEVER ENOUGH.

WELL, JUST BEFORE YOU CLIMB ALL THE WAY TO THE END
OF YOUR TETHER, CONSIDER THIS. YOU ARE NOW THE LUCKY
OWNER OF F**K UP THIS BOOK, THE PERFECT ANTIDOTE
TO THE STRESSES AND STRAINS OF THE MODERN WORLD.
YOU'LL GET TO PUNCH IT, KICK IT, HIT IT WITH A HAMMER,
CUT IT INTO PIECES (HOW SMALL IS YOUR CALL), REASSESS
SOME OF YOUR DEEPEST DESIRES, YOUR DEEPEST FEARS,
YOUR DARKEST SHADOWS.

AND ONCE YOU'VE FINISHED EXACTING A TERRIBLE
REVENGE ON THIS POOR INNOCENT BOOK, YOU WILL FEEL
BETTER. YOU WILL ACHIEVE A NEW PERSPECTIVE ON
YOUR LIFE. YOU WILL HAVE A NEW SET OF GOALS FOR THE
FUTURE. AND YOU WILL HAVE A BOOK FULL OF STUFF WHICH,
IF YOU'VE DONE IT PROPERLY, YOU SHOULD NEVER, EVER,
SHOW TO ANOTHER LIVING HUMAN BEING. UNLESS IT'S YOUR
THERAPIST AND THERE'S AN OATH OF SECRECY.

ENJOY!

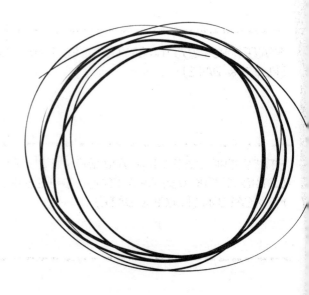

STATE YOUR NAME (YOU MAY CHOOSE A NOM DE PLUME)

STATE YOUR OCCUPATION

STATE THE OCCUPATION YOU'D LIKE TO BE DOING

STATE THE REASON WHY YOU'RE NOT IN THAT OCCUPATION

ON A SCALE OF 1 TO 10 WHERE 1 IS MILD AND 10 IS SEVERE,
STATE YOUR NORMAL LEVEL OF EXISTENTIAL ANGST

STATE THE LAST TIME YOU WERE TRULY CHILLED OUT
(PLACE & DATE)

STATE THE LAST TIME YOU WERE TRULY CHILLED OUT
WITHOUT THE USE OF ALCOHOL, DRUGS OR PRESCRIPTION
MEDICATION (PLACE & DATE)

BEEN A WHILE... ?

OK, IT'S TIME TO

F**K

UP

THIS

BOOK

INSTRUCTIONS

1. READ THE QUESTIONS OR INSTRUCTIONS

2. CAREFULLY COMPLETE EACH SECTION

3. ASSESS THE MATERIAL YOU HAVE WRITTEN

4. AH, F**K IT, JUST DO ANYTHING YOU LIKE - RULES ARE FOR OTHER PEOPLE...

5. BUT PLEASE NOTE THAT ANYTHING YOU DO IS AT YOUR OWN RISK AND ANY INJURY OR UNPLEASANT OR UNFORESEEN CONSEQUENCE AS A RESULT OF YOUR ACTIONS IS ENTIRELY YOUR OWN RESPONSIBILITY. ALWAYS DESTROY RESPONSIBLY. AND CAREFULLY.

DON'T FORGET!

THIS IS YOUR BOOK TO DO WITH AS YOU PLEASE. ANYTIME YOU FEEL THE NEED TO HIT, PUNCH, KICK, RIP, TEAR OR VANDALISE THIS BOOK IN ANY WAY WHATEVER, WHENEVER ANYTHING HERE IRRITATES YOU, THEN PLEASE GO FOR IT. IT WILL MAKE YOU FEEL BETTER.

WORK

HAD A BAD DAY?

OK, LET'S GET STRAIGHT DOWN TO IT.
IF YOU'VE HAD A SHITTY DAY AT WORK,
GET A SMALL TO MEDIUM SIZED HAMMER
AND SMASH THE CRAP OUT OF THIS
PAGE UNTIL YOU FEEL BETTER.

Note: try not to
fuck up this book completely
or you'll need to buy another one to continue.

On second thoughts... do your worst

WORK WORK WORK

WRITE DOWN THE THREE THINGS YOU **LOVE** MOST ABOUT YOUR JOB...

1.

2.

3.

You can leave this page blank if it's not going so well

LOVING YOUR JOB?

WRITE DOWN THE THREE THINGS YOU **HATE** MOST ABOUT
YOUR JOB...

1.

2.

3.

If there's any blank space left on this page then you can move on to
Section 2 if you want to.

KEEP YOUR FRIENDS CLOSE, AND YOUR COLLEAGUES CLOSER

NAME THE THREE PEOPLE AT WORK YOU DISLIKE MOST AND SAY WHY:

1.

REASON

2.

REASON

3.

REASON

If you need more space for your answers, continue on a separate sheet of paper, or a large notebook, or a lever arch file if you work in a big organisation or things are really bad.

Optional: if things are really bad then tear out this page and either a) jump up and down on it until you feel better or b) rip it to shreds or c) burn it (carefully and in a controlled way that won't harm people, property or animals.)

GET IT OFF YOUR CHEST

WHAT WOULD YOU LIKE TO SAY TO YOUR
COLLEAGUES IF THERE WERE NO CONSEQUENCES
AND YOU COULD SAY WHAT YOU **REALLY** THINK?

1. DEAR _____

2. DEAR _____

3. DEAR _____

*Work.*23

DOT-TO-DOT FUN?

COMPLETE THESE DOT-TO-DOT DRAWINGS.

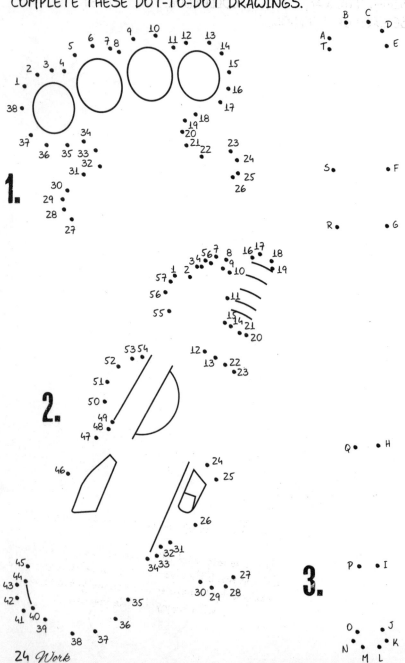

1.

2.

3.

BUT MAYBE NOT FUN FOR?

ASSIGN THE NAME OF THE COLLEAGUE YOU'D MOST LIKE TO USE EACH OF THEM ON.

1.

2.

3.

Note: don't actually do this. They're not worth it.

If you've left most of this blank then thank your lucky stars. Either you work on your own or you're really lucky to have such a decent group to work with. Enjoy it while you can.

COLOUR ME IN

FILL IN THIS BOX IN THE COLOUR THAT BEST DEMONSTRATES YOUR NORMAL MOOD AT WORK. FEEL FREE TO USE HATCHING OR SHADING AS APPROPRIATE, OR SOLID COLOUR IF YOU FEEL STRONGLY ABOUT IT. YOU CAN EVEN USE BLOOD, SWEAT AND TEARS (AT YOUR OWN RISK).

If you used solid black, go back to page 19 and smash the crap out of this book with your hammer of choice. Should make you feel better for a while. If not, consider seeking medical help or getting another job.

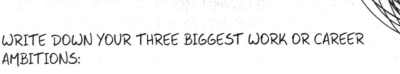

WHEN I GROW UP, I WANT TO BE...

WRITE DOWN YOUR THREE BIGGEST WORK OR CAREER AMBITIONS:

1.

2.

3.

ASTRONAUT, PRINCESS, FIREFIGHTER?

WRITE DOWN THE THREE THINGS YOU'RE LEAST LIKELY TO DO IN YOUR WORK/CAREER.

1.

2.

3.

NB If this list matches the last one then it's time to come up with some new goals. Ditto if you're of a certain age and rock star, Formula 1 driver or supermodel still feature on your list. It's time to re-evaluate.

PICTURE ME HAPPY

DRAW A PICTURE OF YOU DOING THE KIND OF WORK YOU
THINK WOULD BE PERFECT FOR YOU. PLEASE NOTE THAT
THIS PAGE IS OPTIONAL IF YOU:

A) HAVE RETIRED
B) WORK EVEN THOUGH YOU DON'T HAVE TO
C) HAVE RECENTLY COME INTO A SUBSTANTIAL LEGACY
D) ARE A LOTTERY WINNER (WITH A MINIMUM WINNING
TICKET OF £1M WITHIN THE LAST THREE YEARS)

ARE YOU A GENIUS?

DRAW A PERFECT FREEHAND CIRCLE HERE IN PEN:

If your circle is perfect, consider giving up your day job and becoming an artist. You may be a genius. But try and do a really nice painting too and sell it for proper money before you take this step. If your circle looks shaky, oval or the ends don't meet, then best stick to something you can do. If this angers you, punch this page hard (at your own risk).

THE CIRCLE OF LIFE

OK, EVERYONE DESERVES A SECOND CHANCE. DRAW ANOTHER CIRCLE HERE TO SEE IF YOU CAN GET IT RIGHT THIS TIME TO PROVE YOUR GENIUS.

If it's the same as last time, cheer yourself up by drawing a smiley face in your circle. Or a grumpy one if you prefer or if it will make you happier.

BEST DAY EVER!

DESCRIBE THE BEST THING THAT'S EVER HAPPENED TO YOU IN YOUR WORKING LIFE.

You're sure that's definitely the best thing ever? If, after due consideration, this maybe isn't all that amazing, describe how this makes you feel.

WRITE SOMETHING HERE

WRITE THE FIRST PAGE OF YOUR NOVEL HERE

...IT WAS IN THE SHADOW...

Work 33

WRITE SOME MORE HERE

WRITE THE SECOND PAGE OF YOUR NOVEL HERE. IF YOU HAVEN'T MANAGED TO COMPLETE THE FIRST PAGE THEN MAYBE IT'S TIME TO GET REAL, GIVE UP ON THIS DREAM AND GET ON WITH ENJOYING THE REST OF YOUR LIFE?

But don't be too hard on yourself. Everyone thinks they can write but very little of it is worth reading. And even fewer writers make enough money to actually live on. They may have artistic satisfaction and the knowledge that they have, in some small way, left the world a legacy that may or may not be forgotten in years to come, but hey, so what?

MY INCREDIBLY FANTASTIC NEW BUSINESS IDEA

YOU'VE ALWAYS WANTED TO START YOUR OWN BUSINESS? OK, THIS ONE'S FOR YOU. SELL IT HERE. MAKE IT CONVINCING. OR PRETEND THIS PAGE IS YOUR BANK MANAGER, WHO'S TIGHTER THAN A GNAT'S ASS, AND FIND A WAY TO GET THEIR ATTENTION. SELL THE CRAP OUT OF IT.

SO, IN NO MORE THAN 100 WORDS, WHAT'S YOUR BIG IDEA FOR A NEW BUSINESS?

DOING THE BUSINESS

WHO NEEDS THIS PRODUCT OR SERVICE?

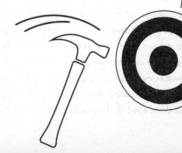

If you can't think of anyone, beat this page up.

ANSWER YES OR NO TO THE FOLLOWING QUESTIONS:

ARE YOU THE BEST PERSON TO DELIVER IT?

DO YOU HAVE THE SKILLS NECESSARY TO MAKE THIS WORK?

DO YOUR FRIENDS AND FAMILY THINK YOU'RE MAD?

DO YOU LOVE WORKING LONG HOURS?

DO YOU LOVE WORKING LONG HOURS FOR VERY LITTLE MONEY?

DO YOU LOVE RED TAPE AND FILLING IN FORMS?

DO YOU LOVE PAYING TAX EVEN IF YOU DON'T SEEM TO EARN AS MUCH AS THE TAXMAN IS GETTING?

If you've answered YES to most of these questions then running your own business really could be for you. It's now time to get a proper business plan together and beat the shit out of yourself until you retire or go bust. Please note, however, that you may never be able to retire because you probably won't have put enough money aside from your meagre earnings. On the upside, retirement and old age can be really crap anyway. And working for yourself can be great, despite the downsides. And if it works out, it will definitely feel good.

Work 37

Summary
WORK AND YOU

IF YOU'VE COMPLETED THIS SECTION AND YOUR COPY OF F**K UP THIS BOOK IS STILL MOSTLY IN ONE PIECE THEN YOU SHOULD NOW KNOW:

IF YOU LIKE YOUR JOB

IF YOU LIKE ANY OF THE PEOPLE YOU WORK WITH

WHAT SORT OF OTHER WORK YOU MIGHT BE GOOD AT

IF YOU CAN EITHER DRAW OR WRITE

IF YOU SHOULD REALLY BE THINKING ABOUT STARTING YOUR OWN BUSINESS

ULTIMATE GOAL: IF YOU CAN MAKE ENOUGH MONEY TO PAY FOR EVERYTHING YOU NEED BY DOING SOMETHING YOU LOVE, THEN YOU MAY BE WORKING BUT YOU'LL NEVER HAVE A JOB.

LOVE
AND
RELATIONSHIPS

I LOVE YOU BECAUSE?

WRITE DOWN THE THREE THINGS YOU LOOK FOR IN
YOUR IDEAL PARTNER. AND, FOR ONCE IN YOUR LIFE, BE
COMPLETELY HONEST - THIS IS JUST BETWEEN YOU AND
YOUR NEW BFF, F**K UP THIS BOOK.

1.

2.

3.

I ♡
LOVE
YOU

I LOVE THIS ABOUT YOU!

DRAW A PICTURE OF YOUR IDEAL PARTNER. INCLUDE ANY PHYSICAL TRAITS YOU'VE JUST LISTED. IF YOU'RE NO GOOD AT DRAWING (REFER TO PAGES 30 AND 31 IF YOU'RE UNSURE ABOUT THIS) THEN JUST DRAW SOME RUDE BODY PARTS THAT AMUSE YOU AND COLOUR THEM IN.

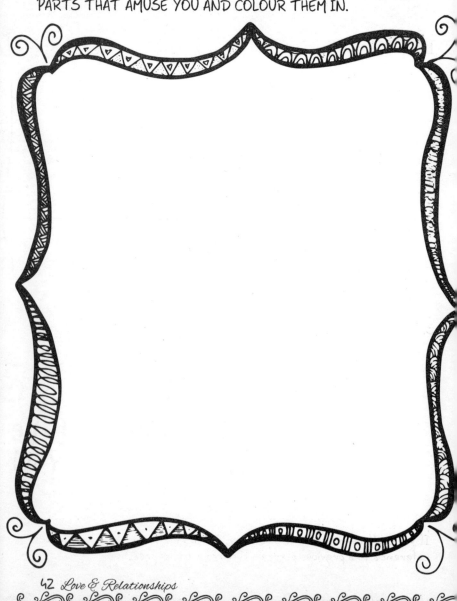

THINGS YOU HAVE THAT I LOVE?

DOES YOUR CURRENT PARTNER HAVE **ANY** OF THE THINGS YOU LOOK FOR IN YOUR IDEAL PARTNER? IF SO, LIST THEM HERE:

1.

2.

3.

If you don't currently have a partner, DO NOT answer this question with reference to a previous partner. It may be too depressing.

I LOVE THAT YOU'RE...

LIST THREE THINGS THAT YOU LIKE MOST ABOUT YOUR
CURRENT PARTNER. IF YOU'RE A BLOKE, THERE ARE SOME
CLUES* AT THE BOTTOM OF THE PAGE:

1.

2.

3.

*Clues for blokes: beautiful, kind, wise, glass half full (of Pinot Grigio), smell
nice, occasionally prepared to sleep with me, reasonably symmetrical
facially, capable of liking me (against all odds) etc.

ANNOYING STUFF

WHAT ARE THE THREE THINGS THAT ANNOY YOU MOST ABOUT YOUR CURRENT PARTNER?

1.

REASON

2.

REASON

3.

REASON

If you don't currently have a partner, please DO make yourself feel better by using a previous partner. And pick the worst one, the one you'd cross the street, or leave the country (if things were that bad), to avoid. If this question annoys you, punch this book in the guts a few times, like a cop with a criminal in a bad B movie.

I WILL FIX YOU

ARE ANY OF THE THINGS THAT ANNOY YOU MOST ABOUT YOUR PARTNER FIXABLE?

1.

2.

3.

If so, great - fix them! If not, why are you still with them?

WHO SAID ROMANCE WAS DEAD?

WHAT'S THE MOST ROMANTIC THING YOU'VE EVER DONE FOR YOUR CURRENT PARTNER? IF YOU CAN THINK OF MORE THAN ONE, WRITE A LIST OF THE BEST THREE. IF YOU'RE A MAN, THEN ONE ITEM WILL SUFFICE.

1.

2.

3.

EVERYTHING I DO, I DO IT FOR YOU

WHAT'S THE MOST ROMANTIC THING YOU'VE EVER DONE FOR **ANY** PARTNER?

Paris ♥
mon amour

If this is different from your answer on page 47, state why you did something more romantic for someone you're no longer with and why you're not making more of an effort with your current partner.

THREE STEPS TO HEAVEN

LIST THREE THINGS YOU REALLY WISH YOUR PARTNER WOULD DO FOR YOU THAT WOULD MAKE YOU HAPPY.

1.

2.

3.

Consider dropping subtle hints to get what you want – anonymous notes, pointed discussions and, if necessary, adverts in the local press or online. If this doesn't work, throw this book hard against a wall. Several times if you need to. An outside wall is preferable to eliminate redecorating costs.

WHO ARE YOU? ??

HOW WELL DO YOU KNOW YOUR PARTNER? SEE IF YOU CAN FILL IN ALL THE DETAILS HERE AND THEN SURREPTITIOUSLY CHECK IF YOU'RE RIGHT BY SLIPPING QUESTIONS INTO GENERAL CONVERSATION WHERE APPROPRIATE.

PARTNER'S SEX:

PARTNER'S DATE OF BIRTH:

PARTNER'S AGE:

PARTNER'S SCHOOL(S):

PARTNER'S UNIVERSITY:

PARTNER'S QUALIFICATIONS:

NAME OF PARTNER'S FAVOURITE CHILDHOOD PET:

NAME OF PARTNER'S BEST FRIEND:

WHICH OF YOUR FRIENDS IS YOUR PARTNER MOST ATTRACTED TO:

If you have answered this question with 'none' then that's either great news, you have no friends or you're delusional. You decide.

...WHO WHO, WHO WHO?

PARTNER'S JOB TITLE (IF WORKING):

PARTNER'S FAVOURITE COLOUR:

PARTNER'S FAVOURITE BAND OR MUSIC:

PARTNER'S FAVOURITE HOLIDAY DESTINATION:

PARTNER'S ULTIMATE HOLIDAY DESTINATION:

NAMES OF PARTNER'S PARENTS (ALIVE OR DEAD):

BIRTHDAYS OF PARTNER'S PARENTS (ALIVE ONLY):

PARTNER'S DESIRED EPITAPH:

The last question may seem odd but it gives a valuable clue about how much you've talked about life's big stuff. It's the bit where a psychiatrist would be stroking their goatee meaningfully, if they were a man or a facially hirsute woman.

If you got all or most of these right then you have been paying attention, which is great news! So why not do something nice today to show how much you love them, but nothing so over the top that they get suspicious about your motives.

FIRST LOVE

WRITE THE NAME OF YOUR FIRST LOVE HERE.

WHAT WAS YOUR FIRST LOVE LIKE? WRITE A SHORT DESCRIPTION OR DRAW A PICTURE.

AND WHAT HAPPENED TO THAT FIRST LOVE? DRAW A TORCH HERE (ANCIENT KIND WITH FLAME RATHER THAN BATTERY POWERED) IF THE LOVE STILL BURNS.

MY LOVE IS LIKE...

DID YOU EVER WRITE A POEM IN HONOUR OF YOUR FIRST
LOVE? IF SO, COPY IT HERE. IF NOT, WRITE A POEM TO YOUR
CURRENT OR MOST RECENT LOVE.

THE BEST OF TIMES...

WRITE DOWN THE THREE BEST RELATIONSHIPS YOU'VE EVER HAD AND WHAT WAS SO GOOD ABOUT THEM.

1.

2.

3.

...THE WORST OF TIMES

WRITE DOWN THE THREE WORST RELATIONSHIPS YOU'VE EVER HAD AND WHAT WAS SO BAD ABOUT THEM.

1.

2.

3.

If this is bringing back bad memories then why not give this page a slap? And if you dip your hand in ink first, you'll be able to gauge later just how hard you slapped it. This should make you feel better and may also create some pretty art in a Jackson Pollock style if you mix your inks.

Love & Relationships 55

DRESS IT UP

DOES YOUR PARTNER STILL DRESS THE WAY YOU LIKE, THE WAY THAT GOT YOU INTERESTED IN THE FIRST PLACE? DRAW A PICTURE OF THE CLOTHES YOU'D REALLY LIKE TO SEE YOUR PARTNER IN FOR A NIGHT OUT. IF YOU CAN'T DRAW, USE CUT-OUTS FROM MAGAZINES OR THE INTERNET.

PERFECT PARTNER

CUT OUT, OR PRINT OFF THE INTERNET, A PICTURE OF HOW YOU'D LIKE YOUR PARTNER TO DRESS UP FOR YOU FOR A NIGHT OF HOT, STEAMY PASSION.

If you can't remember what a night of hot, steamy passion feels like, or you've never had one, study material is widely available on the internet to help with your creativity.

SURF TIME

WRITE DOWN THE NAMES OF THE THREE WEBSITES YOU LOVE MOST, THE ONES YOU VISIT MOST OFTEN.

1.

2.

3.

If you haven't been completely honest here, there's another chance on page 159, in the 'Guilty Pleasures' section.

SURF TIME 2

WRITE DOWN THE NAMES OF THE THREE WEBSITES YOU THINK YOUR PARTNER LOVES MOST, THE ONES THEY VISIT MOST OFTEN.

1.

2.

3.

Put a star beside any of these that match your list. One star or more = extreme compatibility.

OUT & ABOUT

DESCRIBE YOUR TOP THREE IDEAL NIGHTS OUT WITH YOUR PARTNER.

1.

2.

3.

BIG FUN

DESCRIBE YOUR TOP THREE IDEAL NIGHTS OUT
WITH YOUR FRIENDS.

1.

2.

3.

THE CHOICE IS YOURS

IF YOU HAD TO PICK JUST ONE NIGHT OUT, EITHER WITH YOUR PARTNER OR WITH YOUR FRIENDS, WHICH ONE WOULD YOU PICK AND WHY?

NIGHT OUT:

REASON:

If you've chosen a night out with your friends and not your partner, make sure your significant other NEVER finds this book. Unless you really want to be single for a while, in which case you can leave it on the table, open at the right page.

HAHAHA

LAUGHTER IS THE BEST MEDICINE AND A TONIC FOR ANY RELATIONSHIP. SO HOW MANY TIMES IN THE LAST WEEK DID YOU MAKE YOUR PARTNER LAUGH OUT LOUD?

ZERO ☐

LESS THAN FIVE TIMES ☐

MORE THAN FIVE TIMES ☐

HOW MANY TIMES IN THE LAST WEEK HAVE YOU MADE YOUR PARTNER CRY WITH LAUGHTER?

ZERO ☐

LESS THAN FIVE TIMES ☐

MORE THAN FIVE TIMES ☐

If the answer to either of these questions is 'zero' then see if you can achieve both in the next seven days and then write here what it was that made them laugh. Then try to do it some more. Then everyone will be a little bit happier.

ARE YOU FUNNY?

WRITE DOWN THREE JOKES THAT YOU THINK WILL MAKE YOUR PARTNER LAUGH.

1.

2.

3.

Try them out and see if you were right. If not, do something with this book that will make them laugh. Use it as a hat, throw it out the window in a dramatic way or trip over it and fall over in a comedy style (at your own risk).

YOU ARE SO FUNNY!

DID YOU PARTNER LAUGH AT ANY OF YOUR JOKES? IF SO, TRY SOME MORE AND DO IT ALL AGAIN.

MY BEST NEW JOKES

1.

2.

3.

If you discover that you're just not funny, make yourself feel better by ripping this page to shreds.

TEARS ARE THE WORDS THAT THE HEART CAN'T SAY

HOW OFTEN HAVE YOU MADE YOUR PARTNER CRY IN THE LAST MONTH?

NEVER

ONCE A WEEK

MORE THAN ONCE A WEEK

EVERY DAY

ALL DAY, EVERY DAY

If it's not pretty close to 'never', then maybe this is something you need to deal with. Possibly with professional help.

☺ ☺ ☺ ☺ ☺ ☺ ☺ ☺ ☺ ☺ ☺ ☺ ☺ ☺ ☺ ☺ ☺

CRYING WITH LAUGHTER?

DRAW A PICTURE OF YOUR PARTNER CRYING, OR YOU IF
YOU PREFER. AND ANOTHER ONE OF YOU OR YOUR PARTNER
LAUGHING. PREFERABLY NOT ONE LAUGHING AND THE OTHER
CRYING THOUGH - THAT WOULD BE BAD.

DESCRIBE HOW THESE PICTURES MAKE YOU FEEL.

If you require instant therapy, refer to p19

Summary
LOVE & RELATIONSHIPS

IF YOU'VE COMPLETED THIS SECTION AND YOUR COPY OF F**K UP THIS BOOK IS STILL IN ONE PIECE THEN YOU SHOULD NOW KNOW:

WHAT YOU LIKE IN A PARTNER

WHETHER YOUR CURRENT PARTNER HAS THESE QUALITIES

SOME REAL DETAIL ABOUT WHAT MAKES YOUR PARTNER TICK

HOW YOU REALLY GET ON TOGETHER

ULTIMATE GOAL: IF YOU CAN TRULY LOOK AT YOUR PARTNER THROUGH THIS AMOUNT OF REALITY AND NOT RIP THIS BOOK INTO TINY PIECES THEN THINGS AIN'T SO BAD! WORK ON IT AND VALUE WHAT YOU ALREADY HAVE. BECAUSE THEY SAY THE GRASS IS GREENER ON THE OTHER SIDE OF THE HILL BUT, MOSTLY, IT'S NOT.

I ♥ YOU

HOME LIFE

IDEA

FIVE THINGS I DO AROUND THE HOUSE

LIFE AT HOME CAN HAVE ITS UPS AND DOWNS. LIVING WITH ANYONE CAN HAVE ITS ISSUES: DIFFERENT STANDARDS, DIFFERENT WAYS OF DOING THINGS, DIFFERENT HOPES AND DESIRES FOR HOME CLEANLINESS. SO, LET'S SEE HOW THAT'S WORKING OUT.

MAKE A LIST OF THE FIVE JOBS YOU DO MOST REGULARLY AROUND THE HOUSE

1.

2.

3.

4.

5.

If you're a bloke and you can only think of one or two, it might be time to re-evaluate your contribution.

MY BEAUTIFUL DISHWASHER

DRAW A PICTURE OF YOUR DISHWASHER, STACKED EXACTLY AS YOU LIKE IT. TAKE A PHOTO AND STICK IT IN HERE IF YOU PREFER.

RACK & RUIN

CAN ANYONE ELSE IN YOUR HOUSEHOLD STACK THE DISHWASHER PROPERLY? IF NOT, WHAT ARE THEY DOING WRONG? DRAW A PICTURE OF WHAT IT LOOKS LIKE WHEN THEY'VE DONE IT, OR TAKE A PHOTO AND PASTE IT HERE.

If you feel the need, refer back to page 19 and take appropriate action.

MY GARDENER'S WORLD

IF YOU HAVE A GARDEN, WHAT DO YOU LOVE MOST ABOUT
GARDENING?

1.

2.

3.

If your answers include 'peace and quiet' or 'gets me out of the house' then
this is an excellent release valve in your life. If it's more like 'gets me away
from my partner' or 'I love my garden more than life itself' then you may
need to reassess things.

IT'S A PLANT

NAME YOUR THREE FAVOURITE PLANTS.

1.

2.

3.

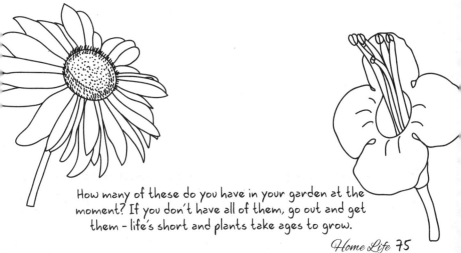

How many of these do you have in your garden at the moment? If you don't have all of them, go out and get them – life's short and plants take ages to grow.

MY GARDEN OF
EARTHLY DELIGHTS...

USE THIS SPACE TO DRAW YOUR GARDEN AS YOU'D LIKE TO
SEE IT. THE FANTASY VERSION WITH PONDS, WATERFALLS
AND A SUMMER HOUSE - OR MAYBE EVEN A SWIMMING POOL
LIKE THE ONE AT THE MARINA SANDS IN SINGAPORE.

DO IT YOURSELF

DOES ANYONE DO DIY IN YOUR HOUSE? IF SO, WHO?

LIST THE LEAST FAVOURITE DIY JOBS, EITHER DONE BY YOU OR BY YOUR PARTNER.

1.

2.

3.

Does DIY make you angry. OK – get a hammer & chisel and make some serious dents in this page.

SIGNATURE DISHES

WHO DOES THE COOKING IN YOUR HOUSE? IF IT'S YOUR
PARTNER, OR ONE OF YOUR FLATMATES, LIST YOUR
FAVOURITE MEALS HERE:

1.

2.

3.

NOW STATE HONESTLY IF YOU STILL PRAISE
THIS PERSON WHEN THEY SERVE THESE
MEALS TO YOU.

PLATE IT UP

LIST THE THREE MEALS YOU COOK MOST REGULARLY.

1.

2.

3.

BEING TRUTHFUL, ARE THESE ANY GOOD?

If the answer to this is no, then think about
coming up with some new ideas. You don't even
have to buy a cookbook anymore, the internet is
crammed with great free stuff

IF JAMIE & NIGELLA CAN DO IT

LIST THREE NEW RECIPES HERE AND COOK THEM ALL
SOMETIME IN THE NEXT MONTH.

1.

2.

3.

When you've cooked them, write down a score out of
ten next to the recipe. If it's less than 7/10 then score
it out and find something new to replace it with. Once
you have three more recipes then you've doubled your
repertoire. And it's nearly a whole week's worth of food.
On the seventh day, eat out!

SEXY EXES?

EX-PARTNERS CAN BE A SOURCE OF IRRITATION IN ANY HOUSEHOLD. SO, HOW MANY OF YOUR EXES ARE YOU STILL IN REGULAR CONTACT WITH?

IF YOU HAVE A PARTNER, HOW OFTEN DOES THIS CAUSE ARGUMENTS?

DESCRIBE THE MOST COMMON ARGUMENT YOU HAVE ABOUT THIS.

If you've written a lot here, you may want to re-evaluate this part of your life. Have you never seen the Jeremy Kyle Show? Try jumping up and down on this book if this question is making your blood boil.

LOSING CONTROL

WHAT TO WATCH ON TELLY CAN BE ANOTHER PROBLEMATIC
AREA IN THE HOME. LIST YOUR THREE FAVOURITE TV SHOWS:

1.

2.

3.

LIST YOUR PARTNER OR FLATMATES' THREE FAVOURITE
TV SHOWS:

1.

2.

3.

If you have a partner, are any of
these the same? Any idea why not?

THIS SPORTING LIFE

DO YOU FIND THAT YOU'D RATHER WATCH SPORT ON TV THAN DO THINGS AROUND THE HOUSE? IF SO, LIST THE 20 (OR MORE) SPORTS THAT WOULD STOP YOU GETTING OFF THE SOFA AND DOING SOMETHING ELSE.

1.   11.

2.   12.

3.   13.

4.   14.

5.   15.

6.   16.

7.   17.

8.   18.

9.   19.

10.   20.

If you've taken this question seriously then chances are you're a bloke. And you may be getting your ear chewed pretty regularly if you have a partner, with good reason. Just saying...

ARGHHHH! (This one's for people with live-in partners)

LIST THE FIVE MOST FRUSTRATING THINGS ABOUT YOUR PARTNER.

1.

2.

3.

4.

5.

RANDOM ANSWERS (Part 1)

DID THE PREVIOUS ANSWER CONTAIN ANY OF THE FOLLOWING:

UNREASONABLE BEHAVIOUR WITH NO OBVIOUS CAUSE

TALKING TOO LONG ON THE PHONE

NAGGING

TURNING UP THE THERMOSTAT TO TROPICAL

ALWAYS DOING LAUNDRY AND COMPLAINING ABOUT IT

SOMETIMES GETTING TOO DRUNK ON A NIGHT OUT

NEVER LISTENING TO WHAT YOU SAY

REMEMBERING EVERY DETAIL OF EVERY ARGUMENT YOU EVER HAD

CRYING WITH FRUSTRATION AT YOUR STUPIDITY

RANDOM ANSWERS (Part 2)

OR ANY OF THESE?

SUPER CONTROLLED BEHAVIOUR TO THE POINT OF BEING CONTROLLING

SHOUTING 'PHONE!' LOUDLY WHEN THE HOUSE PHONE RINGS BUT NEVER ANSWERING IT BECAUSE 'IT WON'T BE FOR ME'

IGNORING EVERYTHING YOU SAY AND MUMBLING 'HMM' EVERY SO OFTEN TO FEIGN INTEREST

KEEPING THE THERMOSTAT JUST ABOVE GLACIAL IN WINTER

NEVER DOING LAUNDRY

ALWAYS GETTING TOO DRUNK ON A NIGHT OUT

NEVER REMEMBERING ANYTHING IMPORTANT

LOOKING AT YOU IN A WAY THAT COULD BE DESCRIBED AS 'DUMB INSOLENCE'

LEAVING THE TOILET SEAT UP OR 'SPRINKLING'

SNORING LOUDLY DESPITE BEING ELBOWED IN THE RIBS

BEING A 'SNORING DENIER'

The items listed here are, of course, wild generalisations, and no-one will experience all of these issues. What, you do? Really? All of them? Even if you only have a few of them to deal with, they can be really annoying, right? And chances are that if you felt more aligned to page 86 then you're male and if page 87 rings a bell then you're more likely to be female, in the case of a male-female relationship. And, although annoying, these items appear to be 'normal' in many relationships. Ok, go on, do something bad to this book and feel better...

Summary
HOME LIFE

IF YOU'VE COMPLETED THIS SECTION AND YOUR COPY OF F**K UP THIS BOOK IS STILL IN ONE PIECE THEN YOU SHOULD NOW KNOW:

ALL ABOUT THE GOOD THINGS AND THE BAD THINGS THAT ARE GOING ON IN YOUR OWN HOME EVERY SINGLE DAY OF THE YEAR

THAT YOU MAY NEED A UN PEACEKEEPING FORCE TO SORT THINGS OUT, BUT THEY USE A LOVELY COLOUR OF BLUE

THAT IGNORING ISSUES DOESN'T MEAN THEY GO AWAY - THEY JUST GET TOUGHER TO DEAL WITH. WHICH IS NOT GOOD.

ULTIMATE GOAL: DEAL WITH THE THREE THINGS THAT YOU THINK ANNOY YOUR PARTNER/FLATMATE(S) MOST ABOUT YOU. AND TRY TO GET THEM TO DO THE SAME. IT'LL MAKE EVERYONE'S LIFE BETTER.

AND SAY THANK YOU WHEN STUFF GETS DONE FOR YOU. TAKING STUFF FOR GRANTED ALL THE TIME - PARTICULARLY IF YOU HAVE A PARTNER - IT REALLY IS TAKING THE PISS.

CARS
DRIVING
AND
TRANSPORT

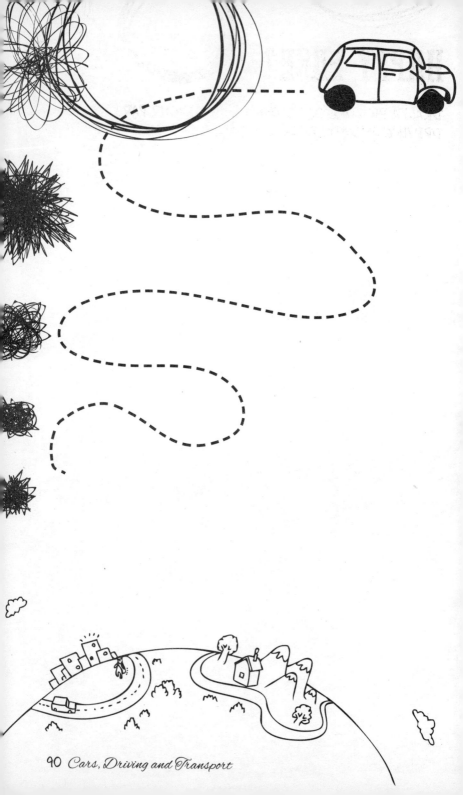

HAPPY FACE?

DRAW A PICTURE OF YOUR FACE WHEN YOUR PARTNER IS DRIVING AND YOU'RE IN THE PASSENGER SEAT.

YOU SHOULD SEE YOUR FACE!

IN THE PREVIOUS PICTURE, ARE YOU:

LAUGHING

SMILING

NEUTRAL

FROWNING

ANGRY

CRYING

WHY DO YOU THINK THIS IS?

BACK SEAT DRIVING

WHEN YOU'RE NOT DRIVING, DO YOU FIND YOURSELF OFFERING HELPFUL ADVICE AND SUGGESTIONS TO YOUR PARTNER? IF SO, WHAT ARE THE THREE MOST COMMON BITS OF ADVICE OR SUGGESTIONS YOU OFFER?

1.

2.

3.

IF I WANT YOUR ADVICE?

HOW IS YOUR ADVICE NORMALLY RECEIVED?

1. VERY WELL, WITH A CHEERY 'THANK YOU'.

2. MORE NEUTRALLY, WITH NO INVITATION TO CONTRIBUTE FURTHER.

3. FROSTILY, WITH A 'COMMENT'.

4. ANGRILY, WITH A DEFINITE INVITATION TO 'SHUT YOUR FACE'.

5. THE CAR GETS STOPPED AND YOU ARE INVITED TO LEAVE.

...I'LL ASK FOR IT!

WHEN YOU'RE DRIVING, DRAW A PICTURE OF YOUR FACE
WHEN OFFERED ADVICE BY YOUR PARTNER

HAPPY FACE (Part 2)?

IN THE PREVIOUS PICTURE, ARE YOU:

LAUGHING

SMILING

NEUTRAL

FROWNING

ANGRY

CRYING

WHY DO YOU THINK THIS IS?

If you've answered 'angry' or 'crying' here, take
this book outside and run over it with your car
until you feel better.

IF I WANT YOUR ADVICE (Part 2)?

WHEN YOU'RE DRIVING, DO YOU FIND YOURSELF WELCOMING HELPFUL ADVICE AND SUGGESTIONS FROM YOUR PARTNER? IF SO, WHAT ARE THE THREE MOST COMMON BITS OF ADVICE OR SUGGESTIONS YOU LIKE TO RECEIVE?

1.

2.

3.

...I'LL ASK FOR IT (Part 2)!

HOW DO YOU NORMALLY RECEIVE ADVICE?

1. VERY WELL, WITH A CHEERY 'THANK YOU'.

2. MORE NEUTRALLY, WITH NO INVITATION TO CONTRIBUTE FURTHER.

3. FROSTILY, WITH A 'COMMENT'.

4. ANGRILY, WITH A DEFINITE INVITATION TO THEM TO 'SHUT YOUR FACE'.

5. YOU STOP THE CAR AND INVITE THEM TO LEAVE.

YOU'RE A COMPLETE F*@!ING A&*!H+LE!!!

WHEN ANOTHER DRIVER CUTS YOU UP ON THE ROAD, DISPLAYS POOR ROAD MANNERS OR GENERALLY BAD DRIVING, IT'S HARD NOT TO REACT. WRITE THE THREE MOST COMMON THINGS YOU SHOUT AT OTHER DRIVERS:

1.

2.

3.

If even thinking about this has annoyed you or made you angry, shout these things at this book until you feel better.

RUE DE REMARKS

DID YOUR PREVIOUS ANSWERS INCLUDE ANY OR ALL OF THE FOLLOWING:

IF YOU CAN'T DRIVE, GET THE BUS!

WHY WON'T YOU LET ME IN YOU BASTARD?

I'VE BEEN WAITING IN THIS QUEUE FOR AGES SO YOU'RE NOT GETTING IN, YOU SCUMBAG!

AWW, FOR FUCK'S SAKE, JUST GET ON WITH IT!

GET IN THE RIGHT EFFING LANE!

WHAT IS YOUR EFFING PROBLEM?

PLEASE, NOT ANOTHER HONDA JAZZ DRIVER...!

Any others?

ROAD RAGE

HAVE YOU EVER GOT OUT OF YOUR CAR TO REMONSTRATE WITH ANOTHER DRIVER (OR DRIVERS)? IF SO, WRITE A SHORT PARAGRAPH DESCRIBING THE INCIDENT HERE.

ANGER MANAGEMENT

LOOKING BACK, WAS THIS BIG OR CLEVER?

WERE THERE ANY LEGAL REPERCUSSIONS?

AND WOULD YOU DO IT AGAIN?

If the answers above
are 'yes', it may be time
to consider an anger
management course.

HOW AM I DRIVING?

HAVE YOU EVER PHONED ANY OF THE 'HOW AM I DRIVING?'
PHONE NUMBERS THAT APPEAR ON THE BACK OF VANS AND
TRUCKS? IF SO, WHAT DID YOU SAY?

LET ME TELL YOU EXACTLY HOW YOU'RE DRIVING...

IF YOU HAVEN'T PHONED ANY OF THESE NUMBERS AND HAVE ONLY BEEN DENIED THIS PLEASURE THROUGH SHEER INDOLENCE OR THE LACK OF A SUITABLE HANDS FREE TELEPHONE, WRITE HERE WHAT YOU'D LIKE TO SAY TO ALL THE VAN AND TRUCK DRIVERS WHO HAVE BEEN DRIVING BADLY IN FRONT OF YOU BUT HAVE GOT AWAY WITH IT SO FAR.

TIME FOR TRAINING

ENOUGH ABOUT CARS, WHAT ABOUT TRAINS? WHAT IS YOUR FAVOURITE TRAIN JOURNEY IN THE WORLD AND WHY?

SLOW TRAIN COMING

IF THE PREVIOUS PAGE IS BLANK BECAUSE OF A LACK OF EXPERIENCE OF THE ORIENT EXPRESS, THE JAPANESE BULLET TRAIN OR THE TRANS-SIBERIAN RAILWAY, DON'T WORRY. THE 7.10 FROM CROYDON, OR YOUR EQUIVALENT, IS A FINE JOURNEY IN AND OF ITSELF. SO JOT DOWN THE THREE THINGS YOU LIKE BEST ABOUT IT.

1.

2.

3.

If this page is blank because you hate commuting to and from some dingy or too-bright office building miles from where you live, consider starting your own business - it might be time for a change...

THEY NEVER FOUND THE BODY...

WRITE DOWN THE MOST INTERESTING CONVERSATION YOU'VE OVERHEARD ON A TRAIN.

If it's really juicy, consider using this as the basis for your first novel.

LET ME TELL YOU SOMETHING...

WHAT WOULD YOU REALLY LIKE TO SAY TO THAT ANNOYING PERSON TALKING LOUDLY ON THEIR MOBILE ON THE TRAIN WHEN YOU'VE JUST REACHED A REALLY GOOD BIT IN YOUR BOOK, OR YOU'RE PRETENDING TO WORK?

DON'T HOLD BACK...

ON YOUR BIKE

IF YOU COMMUTE TO WORK ON YOUR BIKE, THEN THIS QUESTION IS FOR YOU:

Don't you know it's incredibly dangerous to cycle anywhere near traffic? Most drivers are either maniacs, not paying attention or squabbling with their partners about nothing very much. So good luck out there!

IF CYCLISTS HAVE ANNOYED YOU, GET YOUR BIKE OUT AND RIDE OVER THIS PAGE REPEATEDLY. IT MIGHT NOT MAKE YOU FEEL BETTER BUT THE TYRE MARKS WILL LOOK NICE.

RUN FOR IT!

IF YOU RUN TO WORK, THEN THIS QUESTION IS FOR YOU:

SERIOUSLY, WHY?????

Don't you know it's incredibly annoying to run anywhere near pedestrians? Most pedestrians are either maniacs, not paying attention or squabbling on their mobiles with their partners about nothing very much. Go to the gym like everyone else does a couple of times a year. Just because you have showers at work – you do, don't you? – doesn't mean you have to use them...

AND ANOTHER THING...

WRITE A NOTE HERE TO LEAVE ON SOMEONE'S WINDSCREEN. IT CAN BE ANYTHING YOU LIKE, PERHAPS WHEN SOMEONE HAS BLOCKED YOUR CAR IN, TAKEN UP TWO PARKING SPACES WITH THEIR SMALL HATCHBACK THANKS TO THEIR DREADFUL PARKING, FOR SOMEONE YOU'VE SPOTTED PARKING IN THE DISABLED SPACE WITHOUT A PERMIT AND WATCHED THEM RUN INTO THE SUPERMARKET FOR EMERGENCY CIGARETTES OR MAYBE FOR A PARENT WHO HAS PARKED IN A PARENT AND CHILD SPACE AND THEN GOT OUT WITH THEIR LATE TEEN OR TWENTY-SOMETHING KIDS. VENT YOUR SPLEEN AS YOU SEE FIT:

Summary
CARS, DRIVING AND TRANSPORT

IF YOU'VE COMPLETED THIS SECTION AND YOUR COPY OF F**K UP THIS BOOK IS STILL IN ONE PIECE THEN YOU SHOULD NOW KNOW:

HOW THINGS ARE FOR YOU WHEN YOU TRY TO GET FROM A TO B

AND IF THEY'RE BAD, MAYBE IT'S WORTH CONSIDERING WORKING FROM HOME. AND GETTING EVERYTHING YOU NEED DELIVERED TO YOUR DOOR SO THAT SOMEONE ELSE CAN DEAL WITH THE HELL THAT IS THE MODERN WORLD OF TRANSPORT

ULTIMATE GOAL: IF IT HELPS, SWEAR LOUDLY, SWEAR OFTEN AND MAKE YOURSELF FEEL AS GOOD AS POSSIBLE. BETTER OUT THAN IN.

THE
MODERN
WORLD

MY FAVOURITE CELEBRITY

CELEBRITIES - WHO ARE THEY? AND HOW CAN THEY BE CELEBRITIES WHEN NO-ONE HAS EVER HEARD OF THEM OR KNOWS WHAT THEY DO? IN THE ANCIENT WORLD OF THE 19TH AND 20TH CENTURIES, IT TOOK BLOOD, TOIL, SWEAT AND TEARS TO BUILD AN EMPIRE. IN THE MODERN WORLD, YOU CAN ACHIEVE THIS WITH A PRETTY FACE, A HUNGER FOR FAME, A HUGE ASS (THE NON-DONKEY VARIETY), A SEX TAPE AND THE INTERNET. AND A FEW HUNDRED MILLION PEOPLE TO TAKE AN INTEREST.

BUT LET'S START BY WRITING DOWN THE NAMES OF THE THREE CELEBRITIES YOU LIKE BEST. THE ONES YOU'D REALLY WANT TO HANG OUT WITH FOR A NIGHT. OR ALL NIGHT...

1.

2.

3.

BREAKING NEWS... PERT HOLLYWOOD SIDEBOOB SELFIE

NOW WRITE DOWN THE NAMES OF THE THREE CELEBRITIES YOU ACTUALLY READ ABOUT MOST IN THE QUALITY PRESS (DAILY MAIL ETC). THE ONES WHO APPEAR IN ARTICLES LIKE 'CELEBRITY WOMAN TAKES DOG FOR A WALK' OR 'ACTOR/ COMEDIAN MAN GOES TO WELL-KNOWN COFFEE EMPORIUM AND BUYS COFFEE' OR 'WOMAN TAKES SELFIE SHOWING HER PERT POSTERIOR/ INCREDIBLE CLEAVAGE/ ENDLESS LEGS/ SIDEBOOB (ETC) AND PUTS IT ON HER SOCIAL MEDIA PLATFORM OF CHOICE'.

1.

2.

3.

If the use of phrases like 'pert posterior', 'endless legs' and 'sideboob' annoys you then stamp on this page repeatedly wearing the largest, muddiest boots you have.

WHY ARE THEY FAMOUS?

NOW FULLY EMBRACE THIS CHANCE TO WRITE DOWN THE
NAMES OF THE CELEBRITIES WHO ANNOY YOU THE MOST AND
SAY WHY. YOU MAY CHOOSE UP TO 100.

'K' IS FOR...

IF THE TOP OF YOUR LIST ON THE LAST TWO PAGES WASN'T KIM KARDASHIAN, KANYE, KHLOE, KOURTNEY, KYLIE, KENDALL OR ANYONE RELATED TO THEM WHOSE NAME BEGINS WITH 'K', EXPLAIN WHY NOT.

STATE IF YOU THINK KIM WOULD EVER HAVE MARRIED KANYE IF HIS NAME STARTED WITH A 'C'? AS IN 'CANYE'?

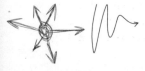

BREAKING BIG

DRAW A PICTURE HERE OF HOW YOU THINK KIM KARDASHIAN GOT HER FIRST BIG BREAK INTO THE WORLD OF CELEBRITY.

If you don't know the answer to this but would like to find out, an internet search for 'how did kim kardashian become famous' will tell you everything you need to know - if you really do need to know. But remember, once you know something, you can never unknow it.

KA$H IS KING!

MAKE A LIST OF THE TOP FIVE SKILLS OR ASS-ETS THAT
HAVE MADE KIM KARDASHIAN A FORTUNE IN EXCESS OF
$100 MILLION.

1.

2.

3.

4.

5.

Note: it's ok to fill in five answers here if you can think of that many.
Kardashian's celebrity is all part of our modern world and you need to be in
it to win it.

SUPPLEMENTARY QUESTION: HOW ANNOYING IS IT THAT
KIM K MUST ACTUALLY BE QUITE CLEVER TO HAVE TURNED
HERSELF FROM A NOBODY INTO AN 'ENTERTAINMENT'
INDUSTRY BASED ON HERSELF AND HER SELFIES?

WANT SOME OF THAT?

TO GET INTO THE FORBES TOP 100 HIGHEST PAID
CELEBRITIES LIST, YOU NEED TO BE IN ONE OF THE
FOLLOWING OCCUPATIONS:

ATHLETE

MUSICIAN

ACTOR

PERSONALITY

AUTHOR

MAGICIAN

HIP-HOP IMPRESARIO

MODEL

COMEDIAN

RANK THESE IN ORDER OF THE ONES YOU JUST MIGHT HAVE
A SHOT AT. OR BUY A LOTTERY TICKET.

SOCIAL INTERCOURSE

SOCIAL MEDIA IS A KEY PART OF THE MODERN WORLD, AND USING IT WELL CAN HELP MAKE YOU A FORTUNE. SO, HOW FAMILIAR ARE YOU WITH THIS FASCINATING NEW MEDIA WORLD? FILL IN THE MISSING BLANKS TO REVEAL THE SOCIAL NETWORKING AND ONLINE PLATFORMS:

F _ _ _ B _ _ K

N _ N G

_ _ I _ _ E _

F _ I _ _ R

_ N _ T _ G _ _ _

V _ _ _ O

G _ _ G _ _ +

Y _ _ _ U _ _

_ _ 5

DI _ _

L _ _ _ E D _ _

_ I _ T _ _ _ _ _

F _ _ E N D _ _ _ R

R _ D _ I _

Answers at the back of the book. If you got less than 10 correct then it's time you took a social media crash course.

COOL STUFF

IF YOU WERE STARTING YOUR OWN SOCIAL MEDIA PLATFORM, WHAT WOULD YOU CALL IT AND WHAT WOULD YOU WANT IT TO DO?

DRAW YOUR LOGO HERE. AND REFER BACK TO 'STARTING YOUR OWN BUSINESS' IF THIS IS DOING IT FOR YOU. OR MOVE ON TO THE NEXT PAGE IF THIS BORES YOU MORE THAN YOU CAN SAY.

I WILL FOLLOW

OK, LET'S HAVE A LOOK AT HOW MANY TWITTER FOLLOWERS SOME CELEBRITIES HAVE. THEY MAY NOT PERSONALLY KNOW ALL THEIR FOLLOWERS BUT WE KNOW THAT THEY LURV THEM SO MUCH. HAVE A GUESS AT HOW MANY FOLLOWERS THESE GOOD PEOPLE HAVE:

KATY PERRY (musician) ....

JUSTIN BIEBER (musician) ....

TAYLOR SWIFT (musician) ....

RIHANNA (musician) ....

LADY GAGA (musician) ....

JUSTIN TIMBERLAKE (musician) ....

BRITNEY SPEARS (musician) ....

ELLEN DEGENERES (personality/comedian) ....

CRISTIANO RONALDO (athlete) ....

SHAKIRA (musician) ....

######################

TWEET, TWEET!

JENNIFER LOPEZ (musician) ....

KIM KARDASHIAN (personality) ....

BILL GATES (businessman) ....

ADELE (musician) ....

BRUNO MARS (musician) ....

MARSHALL MATHERS (musician) ....

EMMA WATSON (actor) ....

RICHARD BRANSON (businessman/personality) ....

RICKY GERVAIS (comedian/actor) ....

STEPHEN FRY ....
(personality/actor/author/entertainer/comedian and quite possibly musician/athlete as well. It would not be surprising to see him win gold at the Olympics whilst playing violin to a creditable standard.)

#
#
#
#
#
#
#
#
#
#
#
#
#
#
#
#
#

###

YES, REALLY, THAT MANY...

SO, HOW DID YOU GET ON? HERE ARE THE ANSWERS, IN **MILLIONS** (SCARILY):

KATY PERRY (musician) .... **75** ....

JUSTIN BIEBER (musician) .... **67** ....

TAYLOR SWIFT (musician) .... **63** ....

RIHANNA (musician) .... **50** ......

LADY GAGA (musician) .... **50** ....

JUSTIN TIMBERLAKE (musician) .... **48** ....

BRITNEY SPEARS (musician) .... **42** ......

ELLEN DEGENERES (personality/comedian) .... **47** .....

CRISTIANO RONALDO (athlete) .... **37** .....

SHAKIRA (musician) .... **34** ......

JENNIFER LOPEZ (musician) **33**

KIM KARDASHIAN (personality) **35**

BILL GATES (businessman) **24**

ADELE (musician) **23**

BRUNO MARS (musician) **22**

MARSHALL MATHERS (musician) **20**

EMMA WATSON (actor) **19**

RICHARD BRANSON (businessman/personality) **6**

RICKY GERVAIS (comedian/actor) **10**

STEPHEN FRY **11**
(personality/actor/author/entertainer/comedian and quite possibly musician/athlete as well. It would not be surprising to see him win gold at the Olympics whilst playing violin to a creditable standard.)

If this annoys you for any reason, then tear out these pages and bury them in the garden. Recycling is good. Dig a deep hole if you're <u>VERY</u> angry.

NAME CALLING — GIRLS

NOW THAT WE LIVE IN THE MODERN WORLD AND OLD-FASHIONED NAMES ARE BACK IN FASHION, SEE IF YOU CAN PUT THESE IN THE CORRECT ORDER OF POPULARITY IN THE UK:

GIRLS

SOPHIA
EMILY
LILY
OLIVIA
AMELIA
ISLA
ISABELLA
AVA
SOPHIE
CHLOE
ISABELLE
ELLA
POPPY
MIA
EVIE
JESSICA
CHARLOTTE
GRACE
EMMA
ALICE

NAME CALLING — BOYS

AND FOR THE BOYS

OLIVER
JACK
HARRY
JACOB
CHARLIE
THOMAS
OSCAR
WILLIAM
JAMES
GEORGE
ALFIE
JOSHUA
NOAH
ETHAN
MUHAMMAD
ARCHIE
LEO
HENRY
JOSEPH
SAMUEL

*Answers at the back of the book

WHAT WERE THEY THINKING?

AND NOW, THE BIG ONE. CAN YOU NAME THE PARENTS WITH THE FOLLOWING CHILDREN:

KAL-EL ....

APPLE ....

KYD ....

MEMPHIS EVE ....

BLUE ANGEL ....

MOON UNIT ....

DIVA THIN MUFFIN ....

TU ....

NORTH ....

AURELIUS ....

BLUE IVY ....

RANK THEM IN ORDER OF RIDICULOUSNESS.

NOW PICK THE ONE YOU'D CHOOSE IF YOU ABSOLUTELY
HAD TO.

AND LIST THE NAMES YOU'D WANT TO CALL YOUR OWN
CHILDREN IF YOU WEREN'T RESTRICTED BY TEDIOUS
SOCIAL CONVENTION AND ENDLESS LISTS.

1.

2.

3.

4.

5.

WHAT WERE YOU THINKING?

DID YOU GET THEM RIGHT?

KAL-EL CAGE .... **NICOLAS CAGE**

APPLE MARTIN .... **G PALTROW** AND **C MARTIN**

KYD DUCHOVNY .... **DAVID DUCHOVNY**

MEMPHIS EVE HEWSON .... **BONO**

BLUE ANGEL EVANS .... **THE EDGE**

MOON UNIT ZAPPA .... **FRANK ZAPPA**

DIVA THIN MUFFIN ZAPPA .... **ZAPPA AGAIN**

TU MORROW .... **ROB MORROW**

NORTH WEST .... **K KARDASHIAN** AND **K WEST**

AURELIUS MACPHERSON .... **ELLE MACPHERSON**

BLUE IVY CARTER .... **BEYONCE** AND **JAY Z**

LET'S PLAY CELEBRITY DYNASTY!

NOW FOR SOME FUN. PICK YOUR LEAST FAVOURITE CELEBRITIES OF CHILD BEARING AGE AND NAME THEIR NEXT CHILD. THE RUDER AND MORE UNSAVOURY THE BETTER.

LET'S START WITH:

1. .... KARDASHIAN
(MUST START WITH A 'K', SO MAYBE 'KROESUS' OR 'KA$H'?)

2. ....

3. ....

4. ....

5. ....

This sort of shit really could happen so why not start your own F _ _ B _ _ K campaign to make sure it does. That's the power of social media... YOU can make it happen.

PASSED CARING?

ONE OF THE THINGS WE ALL NEED IN THE MODERN WORLD
IS PASSWORDS AND PIN NUMBERS. WITHOUT WRITING
THEM OUT IN FULL, LIST ALL THE DEVICES, ACCOUNTS,
WEBSITES AND OTHER PARAPHERNALIA THAT YOU HAVE
PASSWORDS AND PIN NUMBERS FOR THAT YOU CAN THINK
OF AND SEE IF YOU CAN SET A WORLD RECORD.

device/account/website etc   password/PIN

....
....
....
....
....
....
....
....
....
....
....
....
....
....

PASSED OUT?

PASSWORDS AND PIN NUMBERS (CONTINUED)

device/account/website etc   password/PIN

....

....

....

....

....

....

....

....

....

....

....

....

....

....

....

....

....

PASSED ON TO THE OTHER SIDE YET?

PASSWORDS AND PIN NUMBERS (CONTINUED)

device/account/website etc	password/PIN
....	....
....	....
....	....
....	....
....	....
....	....
....	....
....	....
....	....
....	....
....	....
....	....
....	....
....	....
....	....
....	....
....	....

Are all or most of your passwords and pin numbers the same? Makes it so much easier for someone to take complete control of your life. Someone other than your partner, of course.

FIT AS A VEGETARIAN BUTCHER'S DOG?

EXERCISE IS A VITAL PART OF THE MODERN WORLD. WE NEED TO EAT WELL AND EXERCISE HARD TO STAY FITTER AND HEALTHIER FOR LONGER, SO THAT WE CAN WORK FOREVER, LOOK FORWARD TO LOOKING AFTER GRANDCHILDREN WHOSE PARENTS CAN'T AFFORD NOT TO WORK OR CAN'T BE BOTHERED LOOKING AFTER THEIR OWN CHILDREN AND, WITH ANY LUCK, ENJOY A LONG SPELL HANGING ON FOR GRIM DEATH FOR MANY YEARS, CATCHING UP ON DAYTIME TV.

SO, TICK THE EXERCISES YOU DO REGULARLY:

RUNNING

CYCLING

JOGGING

HOME GYM

GYM

SQUASH

BADMINTON

TENNIS

SWIMMING

PILATES

YOGA

ZUMBA

DANCERCISE

HIGH INTENSITY TRAINING

WALKING

WALKING THE DOG

WALKING TO THE SHOPS FOR FAGS

WALKING TO THE CAR TO DRIVE TO THE SHOPS FOR FAGS

WALKING TO THE PUB

WALKING TO THE CAR TO DRIVE TO THE PUB (NOT RECOMMENDED)

GETTING UP FROM THE SOFA TO CHANGE THE CHANNEL MANUALLY

LEANING OVER FOR THE REMOTE CONTROL TO CHANGE THE CHANNEL

TURNING THE PAGES OF A NEWSPAPER LOOKING FOR A BUNGALOW WITH NO STAIRS

There's no shame in any of these, but if you were pretty far down the list before you found anything you actually do – rather than what you used to do once upon a time – then it might be worth stepping this up a bit before you seize up completely. Exercise wisely, of course, especially if the sofa has a visible imprint of your backside/pert posterior.

THE POWER IS IN YOUR HANDS

AND FINALLY, IF YOU HAD ULTIMATE POWER, WHAT THREE THINGS BEGINNING WITH 'K' WOULD YOU BANISH FOREVER FROM THE MODERN WORLD?

1.

2.

3.

IF YOU NEED TO, CUT OUT ALL REFERENCES TO 'KARDASHIAN' IN THIS BOOK AND DESTROY. THE METHOD OF DESTRUCTION IS YOUR CHOICE.

Summary
THE MODERN WORLD

IF YOU'VE COMPLETED THIS SECTION AND YOUR COPY OF F**K UP THIS BOOK IS STILL IN ONE PIECE, ASIDE FROM THE ODD RIP AND TEAR, THEN YOU SHOULD NOW KNOW:

THAT THE MODERN WORLD IS A COMPLEX PLACE, FULL OF SO MANY THINGS YOU DON'T WANT, DON'T NEED AND THAT HAVE NO PLACE IN YOUR LIFE.

YOU PROBABLY KNOW FAR MORE ABOUT CELEBRITIES AND SOCIAL MEDIA THAN YOU WOULD CARE TO ADMIT TO ANYONE OUTSIDE THESE PAGES.

IT'S UNLIKELY THAT YOU WILL EVER REMEMBER ALL YOUR PASSWORDS. YOU WILL HAVE TO RELY ON THAT FAMILIAR AND FRUSTRATING 'FORGOT YOUR PASSWORD?' BUTTON, AND EVERY TIME YOU USE IT YOU WILL CONFIRM THE YAWNING AND INCREASING CHASM BETWEEN YOU AND THE MODERN WORLD.

ULTIMATE GOAL: KUT OUT THE KRAP IN YOUR LIFE. KARE FOR THOSE KLOSE TO YOU. AND START A KAMPAIGN TO BAN THE LETTER K FOREVER.

ME

IT'S ALL ABOUT YOU

IT'S SELFIE TIME

YOU'VE COME A LONG WAY ON THIS CREATIVE YET DESTRUCTIVE JOURNEY FROM YOUR PAST TO YOUR FUTURE, SO LET'S GET PERSONAL AND EXPLORE YOU. JUST YOU, NO OUTSIDE INFLUENCES, NO DISTRACTIONS. NOW - IT'S ALL ABOUT YOU.

TO GET STARTED, DRAW A PICTURE ON THIS PAGE THAT BEST DEPICTS YOUR NORMAL STATE OF GRACE OR EXISTENTIAL ANGST - ONE HALF HAPPY FACE, ONE HALF SAD FACE.

SWEET RELEASE

USE THESE TWO PAGES TO DRAW A REALLY VILE DESIGN USING THE FILTHIEST, MOST UNPLEASANT SWEAR WORDS YOU KNOW. NOT JUST A FEW LITTLE SWEARWORDS, MAKE IT REALLY, REALLY NASTY AND UNPLEASANT. MEAN IT. OWN IT. FEEL BETTER BY RELEASING THEM INTO THE WILDS OF THESE PAGES.

F*@!ING

A&*! H+LE!!!

HOW MUCH?

HOW MUCH MONEY DO YOU OWE? ADD UP EVERYTHING, MORTGAGE, CREDIT CARDS, LOANS AND ANYTHING ELSE YOU CAN THINK OF. INCLUDE ANY LITTLE SECRETS YOU MAY BE KEEPING TO YOURSELF.

This is one of the most difficult things you'll have to do in this boo Debt can fuck up your life, so be honest and get it all out. Face it confront it. This is the time!

MY STUFF

NOW WRITE A LIST OF YOUR ASSETS. HOME EQUITY, SAVINGS, ANYTHING YOU MAY HAVE THAT'S OF VALUE.

If this is more than your debts then crack open a bottle of something nice and thank your lucky stars. Things could be a helluva lot worse. If not, go back to burying your head in the sand – sometimes a reality check is not what you need.

MY FAVOURITE CHILD

HONESTY IS THE BEST POLICY. IF YOU HAVE CHILDREN,
WRITE THEIR NAMES HERE, STARTING WITH THE ONE YOU
LIKE BEST. THEN STATE WHY THE FIRST ONE ON THE LIST
IS YOUR FAVOURITE.

1.

2.

3.

4.

5.

6.

REASON

If you've really filled this in, what
were you thinking??

MY FAVOURITE PET

IF YOU HAVE PETS, WRITE THEIR NAMES HERE, STARTING WITH THE ONE YOU LIKE BEST. THEN STATE WHY THE FIRST ONE ON THE LIST IS YOUR FAVOURITE.

1.

2.

3.

4.

5.

6.

REASON

Unlike choosing a favourite child, no-one will give a crap about this. I like dogs, you like cats. Who cares?

TO SLEEP, PERCHANCE TO DREAM

OUR BRAINS WORK OVERTIME WHEN WE'RE ASLEEP, PROCESSING ALL THE CRAP WE HAVE TO DEAL WITH, ALL THE WORRIES WE STORE AWAY AND TORTURE OURSELVES WITH BECAUSE WE'RE WEAK AND HUMAN AND CAN'T GET OUR SHIT TOGETHER.

WRITE DOWN YOUR DREAMS ON THESE TWO PAGES AS SOON AS YOU WAKE UP. TRY TO RECORD THE MAIN DETAILS AS ACCURATELY AS POSSIBLE, INCLUDING WHAT HAPPENS JUST BEFORE YOU WAKE UP AND REMEMBER. THESE PAGES ARE JUST FOR DREAMS - IF YOU HAVE NIGHTMARES, YOU CAN RECORD THEM ON THE FOLLOWING TWO PAGES:

DREAM 1.

DREAM 2.

DREAM 3.

DREAM 4.

So what do they all mean? If you've managed
to record dreams here before you filled
in the nightmares pages, then it probably
means you have a healthy, balanced psyche.
Well done!

WITH THE SLEEP OF DREAMS COMES NIGHTMARES

IF YOUR OVERACTIVE IMAGINATION IS WORKING OVERTIME OVERNIGHT TO GIVE YOU NIGHTMARES, RECORD THEM HERE.

NIGHTMARE 1.

NIGHTMARE 2.

NIGHTMARE 3.

NIGHTMARE 4.

If you've filled up the nightmares pages and the happy
dreams pages are still blank, then this could be a
worry. It could even give you nightmares. If you
wake up screaming, get some help. Otherwise,
sort out your life a bit and see if that helps.
Or stop eating cheese late at night.

THE DARK SIDE OF YOU

WHAT'S THE MOST ILLEGAL THING YOU'VE EVER DONE THAT YOU NEVER GOT CAUGHT DOING? INCLUDE ALL ILLEGAL ACTIVITIES, FROM RECREATIONAL DRUGS TO SPEEDING TICKETS, ROBBERY TO SERIOUS UNDETECTED CRIME.

If the legal repercussions would be likely to involve a prison sentence, then seriously, how can you live with yourself? Aren't you even a little ashamed? What would your granny have thought? If it still gives you nightmares, this should be recorded on the previous pages. If it's not, why are you not doing it properly? You're only cheating yourself, and, like a fraudster with a Ponzi scheme, your life is a house of cards waiting for the inevitable collapse.

LIAR, LIAR, PANTS ON FIRE

WHILE WE'RE ON THIS SORT OF SUBJECT, DESCRIBE THE WORST LIE YOU EVER TOLD AND WHY YOU TOLD IT. AND WERE THERE ANY CONSEQUENCES? OR COULD THERE STILL BE CONSEQUENCES IN THE FUTURE?

If this doesn't describe an illegal activity, consider sending it to Radio 2's Simon Mayo show for his excellent 'Confessions' slot.

I REALLY LIKE YOU...

BEING HONEST WITH YOURSELF, WHO IS THE MOST INAPPROPRIATE PERSON YOU'VE EVER MADE A PASS AT?

DID ANYTHING HAPPEN?

DO YOU REGRET IT? IF SO, IS THAT BECAUSE YOU SHOULDN'T HAVE DONE IT, BECAUSE YOU GOT A KNOCKBACK OR BECAUSE SOMETHING DID ACTUALLY HAPPEN?

If your answers made you cringe with embarrassment, you might want to get the hammer out and exorcise the ghost by using it on p19. Or on this page if you prefer. Or slash this page with a sharp knife if that might work better (taking care to only damage the book).

HAPPY MEMORIES

WHO HAVE YOU HAD THE BEST TIME WITH EVER?

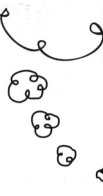

DESCRIBE WHAT YOU WERE DOING.

THINKING BAD

DO YOU EVER HAVE VERY, VERY BAD THOUGHTS? IF SO,
DESCRIBE HERE WHAT THEY ARE.

In the event of these contravening any legislation currently in force,
you may want consider skipping to the next page rather than recording your bad thoughts in these pages. But you should really think about
where this evil has come from.

GUILTY PLEASURES

WHAT ARE YOUR THREE FAVOURITE GUILTY PLEASURES, THE STUFF THAT NO-ONE ELSE KNOWS ABOUT, THE REALLY PRIVATE ONES THAT YOU ONLY DO WHEN NOBODY ELSE IS AROUND.

1.

2.

3.

APPY DAYS?

Cute

HAVE YOU EVER TRIED INTERNET DATING?

DESCRIBE YOUR FUNNIEST INTERNET DATING EXPERIENCE.

BAD MANNERS?

MANNERS MAKETH THE MAN OR WOMAN, BUT WHAT ARE YOUR MANNERS LIKE?

MY BEST MANNERS

1.

2.

3.

MY WORST MANNERS

1.

2.

3.

The lack of manners in the modern world is shameful. Do what you can to make this better.

MY FAVOURITE PHOTO OF ME

STICK THE BEST PHOTOGRAPH OF YOURSELF THAT YOU CAN FIND INTO THIS PAGE.

THE TRUTH BEHIND THE SMILE

WHEN THIS PHOTO WAS TAKEN, DESCRIBE YOUR STATE OF MIND AND WHERE YOUR LIFE WAS AT. AND ARE YOU STILL IN THAT GOOD PLACE?

LOOKIN LIKE SH!T

STICK THE WORST PHOTOGRAPH OF YOURSELF THAT YOU
CAN FIND INTO THIS PAGE.

WHAT WERE YOU THINKING?

WHEN THIS PHOTO WAS TAKEN, DESCRIBE YOUR STATE OF MIND AND WHERE YOUR LIFE WAS AT. AND ARE YOU STILL IN THAT BAD PLACE?

Don't forget you can always use Photoshop to make yourself look and feel better. Like a real celebrity.

It's All About You 165

SCREAM AND THE WORLD SCREAMS WITH YOU

DRAW A PICTURE OF YOURSELF ON A BAD DAY, IN THE STYLE OF EDVARD MUNCH'S 'THE SCREAM'.

ART ATTACK

DRAW YOURSELF IN THE STYLE OF YOUR FAVOURITE ARTIST. OR IN A CAVE PAINTING WITH OTHER ANCIENT PEOPLE AND CREATURES. OR AS AN LS LOWRY MATCHSTICK FIGURE. OR GRIP YOUR PEN IN YOUR WHOLE FIST AND JUST SCRIBBLE WILDLY UNTIL THE PAGE IS SATURATED WITH INK.

SMILE!

DRAW A HAPPY PICTURE OF YOURSELF ON THIS PAGE, DOING SOMETHING YOU LOVE. AND DO MORE OF THIS, MORE OFTEN. UNLESS IT'S ILLEGAL AND APPEARS ON P.154.

PARTY TIME

IF YOU WERE TO PLAN A SURPRISE PARTY IN THE NEXT
FOUR WEEKS, WHAT DATE WOULD IT BE ON? WRITE A LIST
OF PEOPLE YOU WOULD INVITE AND THE MUSIC YOU'D PLAY.
AND THEN DO IT. NO, REALLY, JUST DO IT.

What's the worst that can happen?
If no-one turns up then all the more for
you. But seriously, can there ever be
enough parties?

MY PET HATES

WRITE DOWN ANY PET HATES THAT YOU HAVEN'T HAD THE
CHANCE TO ADDRESS ELSEWHERE IN YOUR F**K UP THIS
BOOK.

1.

2.

3.

Feel free to continue on a separate piece of paper - or a blog if you're
feeling modern.

MY FAVOURITE THINGS

WRITE DOWN YOUR FAVOURITE FIVE THINGS FROM THIS BOOK.

1.

2.

3.

4.

5.

NOW CAREFULLY TEAR OUT THIS PAGE AND FRAME IT.

I NEVER LIKED...

WRITE DOWN YOUR LEAST FAVOURITE FIVE THINGS FROM THIS BOOK.

1.

2.

3.

4.

5.

NOW TEAR OUT THIS PAGE AND DESTROY IT COMPLETELY IN THE MOST CREATIVE WAY YOU CAN THINK OF. UNLESS YOU REALLY WANT TO FRAME PAGE 171. IN WHICH CASE YOU CAN PHOTOCOPY THIS PAGE AND THEN DESTROY IT.

RANDOM ACTS

EMAIL SOMEONE YOU SHOULD HAVE BEEN IN TOUCH WITH BUT HAVEN'T GOT AROUND TO CONTACTING FOR AGES. THIS MUST BE SOMEONE YOU FEEL GUILTY ABOUT, OTHERWISE DON'T BOTHER. PASTE A COPY OF YOUR EMAIL EXCHANGE HERE (IF THEY REPLY).

OR DO SOMETHING NICE, PERHAPS A RANDOM ACT OF KINDNESS FOR A STRANGER, AND DESCRIBE HERE HOW IT MADE YOU FEEL.

Summary
IT'S ALL ABOUT YOU

IF YOU'VE COMPLETED THIS FINAL SECTION AND YOUR COPY OF F**K UP THIS BOOK IS STILL, SOMEHOW, MIRACULOUSLY IN REASONABLE SHAPE, ASIDE FROM THE ODD RIP, TEAR, SLASH AND BURN THEN YOU SHOULD NOW KNOW:

WHO YOU REALLY ARE

WHAT YOU REALLY THINK

HOW YOUR LIFE'S GOING

ULTIMATE GOAL: BE YOURSELF. SOME PEOPLE MAY NOT LIKE THAT. IT'S EVEN POSSIBLE THAT NO-ONE WILL LIKE IT. BUT MAYBE IT'LL STOP THE NIGHTMARES.

AND FINALLY...

SEE, IT'S PROBABLY NOT THAT BAD, IS IT? THINGS COULD BE A LOT WORSE, COULDN'T THEY?

IF YES, THEN GREAT. HOPEFULLY YOU'VE HAD SOME CREATIVE DESTRUCTIVE FUN AND LOWERED THE NUMBER ON YOUR PERSONAL ANGST METER.

IF NO, THEN IT'S MAYBE TIME TO THINK ABOUT REASSESSING AND POSSIBLY GETTING SOME PROPER PROFESSIONAL HELP.

IN ANY CASE, IT'S PROBABLY BEST NOT TO SHOW THIS BOOK TO ANYONE - THEY'RE LIKELY TO THINK YOU HAVE "ISSUES". SO, ONCE YOU'VE COMPLETED THIS BOOK AND ALL THE TASKS IN IT, YOU MIGHT WANT TO CONSIDER BURNING IT (ONLY DO THIS IN A CONTROLLED WAY AND ENSURE THAT YOU AND OTHERS ARE SAFE AT ALL TIMES). AND AS THE FLAMES ENGULF THE BOOK AND THE ISSUES YOU'VE EXPRESSED HEREIN, YOU WILL FIND THAT ALL THESE PROBLEMS WILL DISAPPEAR LIKE SMOKE. OR NOT...

WHATEVER. THANKS FOR **FUCKING UP THIS BOOK** - AND HOPEFULLY NOT YOUR LIFE.

SOME ANSWERS

PAGE 122

F _ _ _ B _ _ K   FACEBOOK

_ _ I _ _ E _   TWITTER

_ N _ T _ G _ _ _   INSTAGRAM

G _ _ G _ _ +   GOOGLE +

_ _ 5   HI5

L _ _ _ E D _ _   LINKEDIN

F _ _ E N D _ _ _ R   FRIENDSTER

N _ N G   NING

F _ I _ _ R   FLICKR

V _ _ _ O   VIMEO

Y _ _ _ U _ _   YOUTUBE

D I _ _   DIGG

_ I _ T _ _ _ _ _   PINTEREST

R _ D _ I _   REDDIT

PAGES 128 & 129

MOST POPULAR CHILDREN'S NAMES.
SORRY IF YOU SPENT ANY TIME ON THIS, BUT THEY WERE
ALREADY IN THE CORRECT ORDER. IT REALLY DIDN'T SEEM
WORTH BOTHERING SCRAMBLING THEM UP. I MEAN REALLY,
WHO CARES?